Kevin —
Hope that you like
some of these poems.
Best Wishes, Andrew

ECLIPSE

POEMS OF DEPRESSION

AND RECOVERY

by

Andrew Jantz

Grateful acknowledgement is made
to the following publications, in whose pages
some of these poems first appeared:

The Boston Poet
The Christian Science Monitor
Iota (England)
Midwest Poetry Review
Parnassus Literary Journal
Polars' Express
Sail Magazine

My appreciation also goes
to the Newburyport Art Association
for its recognition of my work
in its 1997 competition.

Published by
THE NEW ENGLAND PRESS
P.O. box 382174
Cambridge, MA 02238-2174

ISBN 0-9658093-0-7
Library of Congress Catalog Card Number 97-91875

Printed in the USA by

MORRIS PUBLISHING
3212 East Highway 30 • Kearney, NE 68847 • 1-800-650-7888

With love and gratitude to my wife, Joan,
and my sons, John and Tom,
without whose loving support I would not
have survived to write this book.

Table of Contents

I

Darkness Falls

Poison grows in this dark.
It is in the water of tears
Its black blooms rise.

— Wallace Stevens

Song of Experience
(Little Boy Lost)

It is impossible to imagine
what goes through a two year old's
mind when his father
beats his mother
and jams her in a closet.

It is impossible to remember
what the boy feels
when he wonders
without words
if he is wanted.

It is just as impossible
to know what he wonders
when his father disappears
without a word being said
by anyone
ever.

When the child grows up
pain takes shape
in half formed words
that jam in his throat,
causing pain
and more pain
that screams to come out
and can't
find the words.

The Blossom

Fingers part the snow
to reveal
a yellow crocus, caught
in early bloom
by an unforgiving storm,
poised in its
tomb of white —
a rising cry
of color smothered
like Pompeii
by the fallen ash of winter.
Yellow petals stand
bright testament to what
they might have become.
Hands cover them
with snow,
wipe away
the sudden tears.

The Void

The loss of will
to do what
needs to be done

(to breathe,
to love)
leaves a void

which
fills the lungs and
heart where air

and love had been
and causes pain
so dull

it goes unfelt
except
when a child laughs or

the morning sky
awakens
the memory of joy.

New Year's Eve

We are apart tonight
and unhappy in our
separate ways. I could not

don my party hat and smile,
and sit instead at home
smoking cigarettes and listening

to the wind rattle the windows.
You bastard, she had said.
Now she is eating shrimp,

drinking wine, trying
to forget about me.
She will shrug off queries

about me and sip her wine
and as the evening wears on
her singularity will dissipate

in the aura of celebration
and talk. She will bloom
in her natural setting.

And I will sit with my
wallflowers, quietly counting
the petals in my head.

The Sky as Metaphor

This morning the sky burned red
and looked for all the world
like the fiery mouth of Hell.
The scene was set.
I had only to read the lines,
go through the motions
scripted by my life,
to find myself standing
in that mouth, arms at
my sides, head hung
in surrender.

An endless river of black birds
streams overhead.
This is natural.
I am not natural, but I understand
my place and my fate as it is
decreed by the *what* that I am:
a man. This gives me the right
to imagine glorious sunrises and
the right to dread the day.
The right to have faith
and the right to doubt.
But faith and doubt
are two words
for the same uncertainty.
And therein lies
my future.
Meanwhile, the sky has burned
itself out to an ashen gray.
The mouth is closed, for now.
I am left to sip my tea
in fear.

The Pursuit of Innocence

To wander down a street
at night and see
houses lit, shades
not yet drawn, families

at dinner, and turn over
and over thoughts that will not
go away, locked as they are
within, is to illuminate

one's fallen state.
To cry at the memory
of things said
and not said, wounds

inflicted and endured, is to beg
the way to conciliation and
redemption.
To feel oneself

in the blinding beams
of an approaching car is to be
nearer to God
than perhaps one is

in the holy hush of church
but not so near
say, as when looking into
the eyes of a child.

Waiting

Beneath the cloudy archipelago
strung along the sky,
here in my private cell
I yearn to be crushed
or set free
but not remain unchanged,
unchanging,
like the rock beneath
my feet.

A blunt wind, a burst of rain
and the slow birth
of a rainbow are lost
upon my senseless eyes,
as if vision were but a means
of introspection.

To be crushed or set free:
from that seamless
wall of strife and grief
which holds all hope at bay.
I live behind this rock, waiting,
waiting, for the first crack
in it — or me.

The Artistry of Nothing

How does one go about
finding the self?
Does it reside in the flesh and bone,
peering from the eyes —
a wary occupant?
Is it the record of one's life, which,
set in eight-millimeter film,
could be flashed upon the wall
like an old vacation?
Is it a little piece of God
broken off and waiting to be
found in some dark church?
Or is it, rather, nothing —
nothing at all —
giving shape to our lives
as the absence of love
gives shape to one's pain.

Desolation

is easy to find.
In the pages of *National Geographic:*
in the white photos of
Antarctica; in the black
faces of Ethiopians dying

in the dust. It can be seen
through the eyepiece of a
telescope aimed at the moon:
the empty seas, the craters,
the mountains never scaled.

The moon is a cold, godless place.
The Earth is a warm
godless place. Desolation
can be found in city streets:
empty at night or packed

by day with herds of people.
It hangs in the air
like fumes from buses and
cars. It is most easily found
though in the bathroom,

of all places, when one
steps to the sink and sees
two eyes peering out
from the mirror, couched
in recognition.

Greetings from Jersey

Sitting on a curb before dawn
at a deserted strip mall I am
dulled by the slow sound of Muzak
drifting from a speaker overhead.

There's a palpable loneliness
about Muzak playing
all night to a row of darkened
thrift shops and beauty salons.

In the glow of a cigarette
the fringes of my life
disappear in the darkness
of the parking lot.

My wife sleeps alone and
so do I, dreaming
different dreams. I send her
postcards from ugly motels.

In this way do I prove
I exist. For there has been
some doubt in my mind
on this

since I traded my riches
for rags and walked out
of my world, thinking
there was another to see.

At the Unseen Shore

Though full of life
the sea is death. Not
because it steals fishermen
and children (this is but

to kill) but because to stand
before the sea at night
and feel the pull of the
void, the dread of mighty

insignificance, is to face
the edge of existence. Pounded
into submission, the shore slowly
gives itself up in increments

of sand and time — the hourglass
of our days. The ceaseless roar
of the waves masks the feeble,
futile pleas and prayers

for something greater
to stem the tide
and lift us up above
this ebbing of our lives.

After the War

On the flight to Rome,
with the sun and my marriage
sinking behind, I saw Heaven
atop the clouds — endless

ranges of mountains and vales
in colors I'd never seen.
This is the battlefield, I thought,
where the legions of God and

Satan fought the first
and most terrible war.
And as Satan's hosts plunged
through the acrid air below,

all our pain and fear and
grief were born.
I stared through the window
at the sublime desolation

and cried. The fragments
of my marriage were strewn about
like the stars emerging from the
icy air beyond our wing.

I had left nothing behind.
It was all here.
The pilot announced
the beginning of our descent

and as we slowly sank
through the clouds
my insides sank as well.
I pulled the shade.

The ruins of the Eternal
City lay ahead and I knew
I would find the wreckage of my love
everywhere among them.

Rain Therapy

If you lie down in the rain
in the dark and feel nothing,
hear nothing, but the rain,
it can wash away your

troubles like so many words
chalked on the pavement.
Troubles are thoughts and
thoughts are words; the rain can

flush them out. But first
you must open yourself to
the rain. Close your eyes.
Feel it pass through your clothes,

your skin, pounding on your head
and heart, loosening the tears
which turn to rain — which
are the rain. The rain cries

for us because tears are
good at washing out the pain.
Lie down in the rain.
Let the night cry over you.

The Stone in the Stomach

The stone in the stomach
sits there and weighs
the man down.
He feels its weight
as the weight of the Earth.
And the things of this world
bend themselves around
that weight, enlarging it
tumor-like, till the man
can no longer stand
and his legs give out.
Still the weight drags him
down, down into the earth
until the weight of the Earth
and the earth become one
and the man is left
underground, mouth packed
with soil, eyes crushed in
and forever closed.

Summa Theologica

Clouds the color of
pink plates slide behind
the brown wooded hills.
Smokestacks cut the sky
like Roman ruins.
From here the sweep of a hand
could knock the gray pointed hats
off dozens of houses.
But that would be intrusive.
Besides, ugly wooden houses don't make
impressive ruins.
Blasting the plates out of the sky
would prove spectacular, no doubt,
but who would foot the bill
for picking the shards from the trees?
Someone with loads of money
and lots of men. Call in
the Heavy Hitters, the ones with
white suits and gold swords,
the ones who answer to the
Big Muckaluck with the fancy
cloud. He ought to pay anyway.
He makes all the messes.

On the Sudden Death of a Woman

You were not privy to the plan,
the confluence of particulars
swirling around you, unseen,
conspiring to pass your car
before the church the moment
the steeple smote the ground —
smote you —
like God's heavy finger.

An obscene choreography of
red and green lights,
the stop at the store, the births
of your parents,
clicked like tumblers on the vault
of your days — one by one,
numbered.

There are no casual moments;
only these sudden
eccentricities.

Prey

The Fox

A fox had followed its nose
into a trap, a wire cage
with no way out. Now it lay
crouched against the back, as far
from us as its tiny cell
would allow —
a gray knot of hatred.
A stick held to the cage
drew a wild charge of
bare teeth against the wire.

One of the men cautiously lifted
the cage by its handle while the fox
bloodied its nose in vain rage to bite
the hand inches beyond reach.
The man tied a rope to the handle
and swung the cage several times
before dropping it into
the black water of the pond.
We watched in silence while
bubbles escaped from below
and broke the surface like small
mouths sucking air, fighting Death.

After a while they stopped.
The man lifted the cage.
The fox lay limp and bony
beneath its dripping coat,
its mouth relaxed and open.
The man raised it by its tail
and shook the fox till its fur
stood up in wet quills.
He draped the fox to dry

on the rail of a wooden fence,
the pristine coat free of wounds
and blood and any tell-tale
movements to betray
the fox's escape.

The Deer

A light rain was falling
when I raised the shotgun to my cheek
and peered through the cross-hairs
at a whitetail seventy yards away.
The deer stopped and looked my way.
I squeezed the trigger.
The air shattered like the deer's
spine and it fell where it had stood.
I trembled while stillness overcame
the deer, and climbed down
from my tree-stand.
When I was a few feet away
the deer came to life, digging
its legs and twisting its head awkwardly
to look at me.
A strange cry escaped its mouth.
I took aim at its neck and shot
the deer again. Its head arched
backward as if suddenly free and fell
to the ground. All movement ceased.
I poked the animal with the muzzle
of my gun. The deer was gone.

I dragged it to level ground
and turned it on its back.
Its belly was a patch of soft
white fur. I pushed my knife in and slowly
opened the deer to its breastbone.
Warm steam rose up in my face.
I worked my hands through its
innards till I felt the ribbed

rubbery wind-pipe and severed it.
After a few more cuts I turned
the deer on its side and rolled
its guts out on the wet leaves.
The blood was warm on my hands.
I grasped the deer's hind legs
and dragged it to the trail.
Its vacant body
collected rain, which mixed with blood
and puddled the dark cavity.
I was breathing hard.
The rain washed my hands,
but Death stayed with me.
I felt every drop,
saw every leaf,
heard every creature
for miles around.

The Hunter

Stiffened by the cold
the hunter sat motionless
on the small wooden platform
in the tree, waiting for
first light. Silence filled the woods
with an air of expectancy.
The hunter stared into the black
as if trying to discern something
fixed in the vision of his thoughts.
An unseen leaf made its way down
through the empty branches above,
ticking with the irregularity
of a clock winding down
to its final moments.

The hunter blinked
and the tears in his eyes stung
with the bitterness of ice.
His body was poised in its

stillness, bent upon its imminent
task. The silence weighed upon him
like an absence of feeling.
His body drew cold
from the shotgun in his lap
as a tree draws water from the ground.

Almost imperceptibly the trees
around him took form,
and to the east the night paled
above the black hump of a mountain.
Before him he saw
the dim figure of Death smiling.
The hunter raised the barrel
of his gun. He rested the muzzle
against his forehead
and depressed the trigger.
The creatures in the valley
started in wonder.

I Stopped

in Cambridge
at the grave
of Henry James
to see what it

looked like on a
Sunday afternoon
in late Sep-
tember

under a burly
windswept sky when
the first dry
leaves

tumble
against the broad
stones
and the Charles

sweeps by
on its way to the
sea, going home
like me,

going home like
Henry James has
gone —
gloriously

Wind

When enough sadness
and grief rises up
over the towns and fields
it carries

through the trees
and makes the pines
brush the sky in long
slow strokes

and moves the clouds
across the sun in
weary shades of gray.
Leaves on the ground

lift and turn
around and round
with no place to go
as if the motion itself,

the levity of the dance,
could break the spell
and bring them back
to a green life.

Yet they lie down again
one by one,
alone,
almost human in their way.

Suicide, or a Walk in the Woods

What is this strange fascination?
The terminus of my days
has been reduced to a rusted danger sign
ignored too long or seen too much

to be noticed. The significance
of the act has been sucked
of its magnitude. Only the husk
of a paper-thin guilt remains

to remind of the cold consequences.
It is so easily done, this thing.
Traversing this path to a place
I should not want to see.

In the dark it is so easy
not to see. To place one foot
in front of the other, to proceed
step-by-step, each step

harmless in itself. Each tree
I pass stands closer to the next.
The canopy of dark limbs
closes out the sun and moon;

thickens to black. The trail
disappears. In this dark wood
I might stop as if to rest,
as if to sleep, as if

to pretend I do not exist.
Hid from myself this way
I can pretend I do not see
that I am lost for good.

Lost & Found

for Joan

At one a.m. I sat by the pool
smoking cigarettes and
wondering at the stars
which fell from the sky.

At two a.m. I perused the
books lining the study shelves
as if in search
of some explanation.

At three a.m. I walked the streets
of town, reading all the signs
where others had been
in hope of some direction.

At four a.m. I washed down
pills in twos and threes
with glasses of scotch and
scratched out notes to leave behind.

At five a.m. the eastern sky was
stained by the approaching day
and I stumbled to my sleep
only to rouse you from yours.

At six a.m. after slapping and
cursing me to consciousness
you steered me to the emergency
room where they plied me

with that foul black sludge
until I threw up my horde of ills
and found myself in your arms, found
myself in your loving arms.

Amesbury Five

Every stone here sweats with suffering.
— *Camus*

At dawn the screaming starts:
wild, pathetic, as though she
were being butchered instead of
merely waking to another day.
She's in solitary.
The rest of us twist in our blankets
as we have all night, feigning
sleep. At breakfast no one talks
but stares at their pale food or
out the windows at the vast
indifferent clouds gliding by
as if on grease.

Afterwards we stand in line like
communicants to receive our salvation
in denominations of desipramine
and lorazepam.
To shave one must first request
a razor and aver to its safe and
proper use. Like a guardian
angel the nurse's face hovers
next to my harrowed visage in the
metal funhouse mirror. Nicked and
nervous I turn to meet the day.

Here on Amesbury Five the morning
sun drifts vacantly across the windows
like a slowly wandering eye.

Eric

My first roommate is sixteen
and magnetic in his kindness.
He looks like someone's favorite
nephew. When his parents split,
his mind did too and he wound
his way down through expulsion, liquor
and LSD to a place that made him
smash chairs and doors and peoples' heads
before succumbing to the bright promise
of a suicidal dose.
He's all right now, and his worst offense
is standing on the toilet to blow
his smuggled cigarettes into the vent
in the ceiling. On his last night
they catch him and confine him
to our room.

We phone each other now and then.
He likes some of my poems.

Karen

A divorced mother with grown kids,
her life revolves around her lap dog
who understands everything except
why she wouldn't wake one day
and why they took her away.
She insists I eat when all she
ever eats herself is cereal.
We talk about the seductive urge
to lay down and sleep forever.
We say "forever" with a hushed
reverence. A connection is made.

During her last few days here
her wide smile appears along with

the make-up and she speaks with
ebullient joy about the passing
of the clouds and going home
to her dog. Her face is
tight as a balloon.
She worries me the most.

Gary

My next roommate had taken three
hundred barbiturates and made
the mistake of phoning his mother
to say goodbye. This landed him
for a second stint on Amesbury Five. He tries to be funny
but mostly offends.
At four in the morning
he hypothesizes the existence
of God then shoots Him full of holes.
He loves Bach, though.
On his last day a girl with
bandaged wrists breaks down and makes
a scene. "She's crazy!" he shouts
to no one.
He is confined to his room.
I get the bad boys, it seems.

Kathy

Angel of the Ward,
tiny as a doll. She's young
but walks with a limp. She draws
colorful names for every patient's door.
Ten months she's been here and knows
all the ropes. She sees people leave
and come back again and again.
She makes them new signs. She helps

everyone, though they may not know.
In group therapy she stares at the
floor, chin up, and tearlessly
sheds her pain like a worn-out skin.
"God bless us, everyone," she seems to say.

Sam

A bi-polar, all the way.
Tall and strong with a buzz cut
and thick glasses, he walks and
talks with a somnambulistic slur —
a friendly Frankenstein in sweatshirt and jeans.
At night he stalks the room in search
of a place to go. At three a.m. I wake
to find him pissing on the radiator,
then listen as he showers in his clothes.
Another night I wake to find him
sitting on his bed, staring
at me. "Go to sleep," I say. "No," he says.
"I don't want you killing yourself."
A nice guy, Sam is.

Tom

A mild schizophrenic.
Of oriental heritage, he swings
between quietly sitting on his bed,
hands folded in his lap,
to doing scissor leaps about
the room and laughing absurdly.
In and out of bed all day, he
meticulously tucks the blankets
each time he rises.
Once he laid there saying over and
over in a half whisper,
"...stones and sticks, stones and sticks..."

He denied to his parents and his doctor
that he'd begun talking like a baby
during a phone call, then, to me
said: "What if I did? Babies are innocent."

Susan

Before bed, in a darkened room,
they play a recorded thunderstorm
to dampen our smoldering nerves
and we listen to her gentle
sobs mingle with the rain.
Afterward as she flees to her room
I touch her arm and ask
if I can help. She shakes her head
but her eyes belie her need.
We sit in semi-darkness
and as I hand her tissues she talks
through her tears about visiting
the graves of everyone she's ever
loved and how much pain
she inflicted on their lives. I am
helpless before her isolation.
She cries and cries and her tears fall
like rain.

Bob

My last roommate.
Took an overdose and crawled into
his ex-wife's van to die. Now he's here
with the rest of the near misses.
Like the chicken and the egg, he's
not sure which came first: the drinking
or the depression. In the Navy he
sailed the Mediterranean ports and
never made it past the dockside bars.

He wants to make a clean start
with his second wife but doesn't
know where to begin.
He laughs a lot when he's not angry.
He's glad to be here.

Amesbury Five

From our fifth floor sanctuary
in the suburbs we can see the towers
of Boston. In the streets below
we watch the cars motor in silence
bringing unseen people home from
work, school, the grocer's.
Some are happy. Some belong with us.
Most move somewhere in between —
the great middle class, the *bourgeoisie*
of emotion. When we get out
we will vanish in their ranks
and try hard to belong.
Some of us will make it.

View from a Mental Ward

The world outside is two-dimensional
despite the prospects of hills and mills
and scores of homely roofs.

There is a flatness to
the measured spaces between
these panes of glass and the

panoramic clutter spread across
the modest valley. Things
out there exist in a separate

time. A time which moves
in linear moments decreed
by traffic lights and the regular motion

of sun and sky across the shadowed
hills. Here, where we are safety-sealed
for our protection, time moves

in strange rings of repetition,
and objects such as chairs and people
look less as though on film

and more as if that
third dimension forced them into
becoming something real.

Winter in Spring

The sun was a dim light
hung in the coldest sky.
My hands were ice, marbled blue
for effect. My eyes were black.
I could not see that spring had come.
Snow swirled like dust, like ash,
and filled the places where I hid
from myself. I breathed
myself as methane; drank myself
as acid which ate away my insides
and left me riddled with dread.
The self which twisted to reach
some opening to warm air,
blue sky, was too heavy to rise.

Resignation
became the antidote for dread.
When morning broke upon the day
and spread in cold pools of rain, a calm
shrouded me in its pillowy mist and
I could recall bitter words like icicles
piercing my breast, but the pain was gone
and the wounds were numb and I could
think and not feel a thing.
Such sanctuary was found at the cost
of my hands and eyes,
my head and heart. I found a solitude
so inviolate that my children
could not see me, nor I them, inches away.

It is said misery loves company
so I went to a place where my misery
could rejoice with others of its kind.
We sat in circles and choked on our tears.
We stared at our food in silence.

We tried to remember how the grass
had felt beneath our feet,
how we had laughed like children,
how spring had chased the winter.
We tried, but could not remember.

Perspectives of a Dish Antenna

There's a dish antenna
on a wooded hill above town.
Nothing too romantic.
But I remember seeing it
from my bed one morning
ten years ago, a few months
into my marriage.
It was a brilliant autumn
morning and the dish
was framed atop the hill
by the yellow leaves
of an oak outside the window.
I knew I would always remember
that moment because I was
so happy and relaxed and alive.
I was on top of my world, just like
that dish antenna.

Here I am, ten years later,
looking out a window at that
same antenna. Only now it's
February and everything's gray
and brown and I am in
a psychiatric ward because
of an overdose of tranquilizers.
The antenna looks the same.
It hasn't changed a bit.
But somehow
I've fallen down the hill.
I feel I ought to be jealous,
but I'm not.
It's just an antenna on a hill.
It's played no part in its fate.

Ten years from now it will still
be there, doing whatever it does.
If it breaks down, someone
will fix it.
I feel I ought to be jealous.

Of Scylla and Charybdis

What is a man to do
when he is too weak to live
and too weak to die?

He can choose to die
and take a bottle
of pills.

He can choose to live
by standing up
and seeking help.

But after his stomach is pumped
he is left
where he started;

that is to say,
alive but unhappy
to be so.

This is what it means
to be caught between a headstone
and a hard place.

II

The Coming Light

In this night the poet raises his voice
for he has perceived the dawn of a new day.

— Helmut Kuhn

Between Darkness and Light

[Scene: a dimly lit horizon, at dawn. Enter, Darkness and Light.]

Light: See our children, Day and Night,
how they play with one another,
if only for this moment.

Darkness: They are beautiful together,
though so different. Truly
they are ours.

Light: They are us, only less so.
[Hesitates] Their differences
are not so great as ours.
Harmony belongs to them alone.

Darkness: And yet they push each other
even now for control
of land and sea.
They are tireless in their
pursuit. Do they not understand
that so long as the Earth turns
they will neither of them
hold advantage long?

Light: On Earth, at least, we must
reign together — if only
by endless succession to one another.

Darkness: True, in so far as Day
and Night are concerned. But we take
many forms, you and I, and
rarely do we co-exist, if that
is what Day and Night do.
We are wed as opposites,

bound by our differences.
We define each other
even as we fight.

Light: But we do not need
one another. If I were
absent you would flourish, as I
would thrive were you not here.
Light predates darkness
as God predates evil.

Darkness: In the beginning was God,
and you are not He, nor am I
Satan. God created both you
and me, as he did Heaven and Hell.

Light: Hell was forged to catch
the Prince of Darkness as he fell
from God's Light.

Darkness: And Darkness dwelt in Eden
before its corruption, as well
as Light. I am not evil.
I am truth.

Light: [Surprised] That is a lie.

Darkness: Perspectives
are born of light;
they are what appear to be, not
what is, as that sky [points to the horizon]
appears to be ablaze.
In me there are
no perspectives.
Things do not seem: they
only are as they are —
good or evil; ugly or
sublime.
That is truth.

Light: Sin hides in Darkness.
            That is truth as well.
            Sin flies before me.

Darkness: If sin hides in a man's heart
            he is a sinner, no matter what
            he appears to be
            by your light of Day.
            Truth lives in me.

Light: And life and love live
            in me — live
            through me — and what are they
            if not truth? Seedlings
            reach for me
            as they break the earth; men and women
            see me in their lovers' eyes,
            feel me in their flesh and blood.
            And if love begins to fade
            they feel Darkness
            rushing in as a cold wind —
            as loneliness — [pauses]
            as death.
            I radiate from, and shine upon,
            and fill to overflowing.
            I am life. I am love.
            What are you
            but the absence of me?

[Darkness falls silent. Day breaks.]

An Apology

It happened during the ride
in the ambulance
from one hospital's emergency
room to another's
psychiatric ward. Strapped
to a stretcher, head elevated
just enough to see
through the rear windows,
I watched my wife's car
following down the highway —
saw the woman whose life
was bound to mine like an angel
to its wings — and first
glimpsed in horror the monster
of what I'd done
and failed to do.
Clothes stained black from
liquid charcoal thrown up
with sleeping pills and
lorazepam and scotch,
I was crushed beyond
recognition by guilt and shame.
I saw myself from her car —
her shoes — and felt the hurt.
No doubt I'd scraped
the bottom of our lives.
The words "I'm sorry" paled
before the need to make good.
For me the only
atonement would be
to live and love.

Therapy

When all is boiled away
by the heat of pain;
when nothing remains
but the stain of sadness,
then does the self rise up like smoke,
thin and twisting in a breathless void.

These are the essentials:
Consider the self without rancor
for it merely returns the stare.
Consider it as one considers
the body on a slab, to be
sliced and examined in a

neutral light. Stripped of its
power, it will reveal its secrets.
They will rise up like smoke,
like the self,
and smell like fear. The stench
is the surest sign of truth.

Losing Touch

In the psych unit we peeled back
the layers of bandages to reveal
our sickly selves to each other.
No one winced; no one hid their eyes.
We bared our wounds and cried
as we had not been able before.
We knew nothing of each other
but our names and the faces
of our demons. We let them out of their
dark places and watched their ugliness
draw tears with a few honest words,
the slightest touch.
We were brittle bone
draped with the flesh of thin
lives and painted masks,
which had no bearing in this place.
We saw each other through these
transparencies, and through
the days and nights.

Upon our release we scattered
like dry leaves in the wind.
We exchanged cards and calls
the first few weeks and told each other
how well we were doing, but
fear was hiding beneath our words
and we all heard it.
Then we lost touch with each other
and ourselves. We sank back
into our normal lives
and tried to forget.
But we could never forget, just as
we could never completely hide
ourselves in normal lives.
Bones cracked;

emotions bled through clothes.
Some of us failed
for all the world to see.

When I pick up the phone and dial
your number I will feel relief
at the sound of your voice. And if
someone else answers, a daughter
or husband with the mark of grief
in their voice, I will feel
through my tears something of
the profound relief you must have felt
when death closed your eyes.

Of Time and Healing

To sip from a cup of tea
on a dark afternoon
is a simple act

of healing. To hear
the rain upon the window
is a passive act

no less healing.
But to remember by
the ticking of the clock

is to methodically
open old wounds.
Time does not progress

like the hands of a clock.
The past is present
no less than the future,

shaping the present
with course, callous hands —
squeezing much too hard.

Thoughts of Famous Poets

During Therapy at McLean Hospital

The place is not what it used to be.
Once a bastion of those blessed
with money or names
(or both, like Lowell and Plath),
it is now mostly home to the wards
of insurance companies.
And though the grounds are impressive
there is an air of sadness
more prevalent than any
arboreal fragrance.

Enter the minor poet.
It is difficult to imagine this
as a chapter of my biography.
It is even harder to imagine
the biography, unless it is something
scrawled on notebook pages
during all my sleepless nights.
But there are some similarities between
my case and those of my famous forebears:
I've come out of need, and I'll pay
my way in tears.

The Ear on the Wall

[Scene: a psychiatrist's office. A female doctor
and a male patient are seated, facing one another.]

Patient: What is this strange fascination?

Doctor: You've called it a "lust for calamity".

Patient: I don't know if it's merely
            an urge to take my life,
            or something more. Maybe it's
            a reaction to my staid existence.

Doctor: I wouldn't say your life
            has been staid this past year.
            You've attempted suicide and been
            hospitized twice.

Patient: My life is nothing.

Doctor: That's your disease talking.
            You wouldn't say such a thing
            if you weren't depressed.

Patient: But the disease has eaten away
            my life. It's taken my place.
            When I look in the mirror
            it's all I see staring back
            at me. All the things
            of which my life was made
            were riddled with this cancerous
            rot. My marriage, my faith,
            my career, my values,
            my desire to live.

Doctor: You know depression is curable.
           You have to believe that.
           And when the depression is gone
           your life will return, just as
           spring returns when winter has gone.

Patient: Spring — I remember what that's like.
           This year it made me feel worse.
           Everything coming to life but me.
           I wanted things barren and bleak,
           the mirror of what I felt.
           People thought sunshine and flowers
           could lift me up, but clouds
           and drizzle were better by far.

Doctor: Do you believe
           that you will get better?

Patient: I'd like to believe...
           I want to believe. [Pauses and stares at floor.]
           That's what I always said about
           God and the Resurrection.
           I wanted to believe.
           But when you see the world
           the way I do now, you don't
           believe. You can't.
           I still think about that little boy,
           James Bulger, who was murdered
           in England a few years ago.
           Two years old.
           He was lured away from his mother
           at a mall by two older boys.
           They led him across town
           to a deserted area
           then threw rocks and bricks at him,
           and beat him with pipes,
           and kicked him till his blood
           spurted onto their boots.
           They left him on the railroad tracks

and a train cut his body in half.
And I was supposed to shrug my shoulders
and believe that little boy's abandonment
to terror and pain and death
was part of some great and mysterious plan.
I cannot accept that.
If that is part of God's plan then
I want no part of his plan
or him. God should burn in Hell.
But... I don't believe he exists.
If he does, he's not a "he"
but an "it," no more capable
of love or caring than a cloud
or a soapstone idol. That's one
good thing I've gotten out of this
depression: I've come to know
the nothing that is God.

Doctor: I see. [Pauses.] Have you been having
            any suicidal thoughts?

Patient: Every day.

Doctor: And what do you think of?

Patient: I think of taking pills
            and being washed away forever
            by sleep.

Doctor: How does that make you feel?

Patient: At times it makes me feel calm.
            It's soothing to know I have an escape.
            Other times it makes me feel
            horror and guilt at the pain
            I would inflict on my wife and kids.
            Other times I feel horror and guilt
            because I don't care about the pain
            I would inflict on them.

And sometimes it frightens me.
I feel as if I'm stalking myself,
waiting for that moment
when I drop my guard to push
myself over the edge.
It would be murder
as much as suicide.

Doctor: You would go to someone
or call me if you felt threatened?

Patient: I fully intend to.
What I'd actually do, I don't know.
[Pauses. Looks at floor.]
I think...[Pauses again.]

Doctor: You think...what?

Patient: I think I have a confession to make.
I've been holding something back
from you, and my wife.
I've got 400 milligrams
of zolpidem hidden away at home.
I've been debating for days
whether or not to tell you.

Doctor: What made you decide to tell me?

Patient: I'm not sure. Because I have
no intent of handing them over
or telling exactly where they are.

Doctor: But you felt compelled
to tell me about them.

Patient: Yes.

Doctor: I think some part of you
is fighting to live and refuses

to be an accomplice to your
suicide. That's the part
which spoke up just now.

Patient: [Bows head.] I know it's foolish and
             dangerous to keep those pills. I'm giving
             a loaded gun to my own assassin.

Doctor: You're right. You are.
             What exactly do you expect
             me to do with the information
             you've given me? I could tell you
             that you're threatening the well-being
             of your family as well as yourself.
             That you're greatly increasing the
             chance or likelihood of another
             suicide attempt. That your murder
             would clearly be premeditated.
             But you already know all this.
             It's up to you to decide
             how to act. The responsibility
             is yours and yours alone.
             You can control your destiny.
             Here's an opportunity to exercise
             the existential freedom you've
             often talked about. But remember,
             with that freedom comes
             responsibility. Whatever
             you decide to do, you are
             responsible for your actions
             and the consequences they bring.
             If you decide to take your life
             then you must also accept
             responsibility for
             the destruction of your family.
             You have a diseased mind.
             Are you willing to gamble
             the lives of your wife and sons
             on the premise that you are

capable of making a sound
decision in your present state of mind?
Don't you owe them — and yourself —
the benefit of the doubt?
Can't you at least recognize
the possibility
that you will be cured
and that you will see things
very differently than you do right now?
Again, don't you and those who
love you deserve the benefit
of the doubt? Do you
hear what what I am saying to you?

[Patient is weeping softly, head bowed. He does not reply.]

Soliloquy

Again, why this strange
fascination?
There is a reckless thrill

beckoning as if this
were no more than an act
to amaze family and friends.

In the glow of the footlights
I mouth the words "To sleep...
and by a sleep to say we end..."

But there is no applause.
Only a sickening silence
which descends like a black curtain

to cut me off,
to cut me off for good.
And in the darkness I hear

the cries of my children
rend the silence
and burn for years in hurt.

A hurt which would never go away,
could never go away,
if I go away.

A Full Moon Rising

over empty trees
on a winter night brings
with it a clarity uncommon
to the light of day.

The moon passes slowly
behind a dark steeple,
mounting the celestial lair
in silence, free of strings

and hopes and little thoughts.
The steeple points in
supplication; the moon
motions like clockwork.

Indigo fills the night,
bathes the distant city
blinking by the edge
of sea and sky. The moon

absorbs the prayers, the wistful
stares, of lovers
and the sad of heart
and sheds its second-hand

light, impervious.
Still, its presence fills
a void, lifts all eyes
to behold our mutual zenith.

7 a.m.

In bed
on a gray morning:
to stare at the woolen
sky,
watch a weak
spot of light grow
brighter and spread —
becoming slowly
a radiant hole
through which great
beams spoke the air —
sunlight forcing
through,
creating shadows,

changing perspectives.

Three Chimneys

When one is relaxed and can take note
of the changing light on the sloped
planes of a roof, the shifting multitude
of grays, the chimneys present
a reassuring form in the fluid
temporality of change. The chimneys stand tall,
rigid, red in their stature of brick.
The roof could cave, the walls and timbers
rot, and still the chimneys would stand,
monuments to themselves. In time
of course they would lean and collapse
like everything else because
nothing but change is permanent.
And yet they stand, these chimneys,
like sequoias, like the great columns of Rome,
lending their brand of grandeur, their ancient
aspirations, to a fragile mind in need.

The Doctor

for Hal Cash, M.D.

Strange how this works.
You ask how I'm doing
and I pour out my ills
like dirt from a bag
all over your office floor.

We sift through it
looking for pieces of my past,
clues to the mystery
behind the depression.
You always find something

to hold to the light,
something I'd missed
or glossed over
in my nervous search.
And if I cry at the sight

your compassion
cradles me in silence.
You dust off the find
and give it to me to hold,
to examine, to assuage my fear.

You're a stranger to me
as I am to myself. Yet
you know me as others cannot.
Somehow in our sifting
we will find enough pieces

to put together a self,
and this self will be me.
You will introduce us.
The pills will keep us together.
Strange how this works.

The Self as the Letter C

All thy passions in the end became
virtues, and all thy devils angels.
*   —Nietzsche*

The Problem

It begins with the grandiosity
of good and evil. *A* is good.
A thinks *B* is evil.

A plus *B* equals self, *C*. The conflict
arises in simple questions:
Can *B* ignore the moral edicts

of *A*? Can he make
his own rules and break them?
Can *B* make a myth of God?

A sits in judgement of *B* and
weighs him down with chains of
guilt. *B* struggles to free himself

and curses *A* to no end.
C is unhappy because *A*
hates *B* and *B* loathes *A*.

C is unhappy because *C* is
neither *A* nor *B*, but only
the sum of both — despair.

C hates *C*, and wants to die.
With the aid of *B*, *C* swallows
a bottle of sleeping pills.

66

A refuses to die;
consequently all three survive.
No one is happy. What shall they do?

The Resolution

C walks alone on a beach
and examines *A* and *B*
in the thin morning light.

C decides *A* is wrong.
B is capable of evil,
but *B* is not evil

any more than *A* is evil.
C realizes *B* is freedom
and is therefore good.

C knows *A* and *B* can co-exist.
C overtakes both *A* and *B*.
C instructs *A*

to relax; to let go;
B, to stop fighting for air.
C stirs some of *B* into *A*

and some of *A* into *B*.
C's guilt disappears.
C knows the equation has changed.

A plus *B* does not equal *C*.
A plus *B* equals something new.
I, perhaps.

The Rains of Clarification

For twelve months the rain fell
even on the clearest days.
The flood rose and carried away
all his valuables
while he clutched and thrashed
in dumb panic,
feet nailed to the floor.
The refuse of his past swirled
beneath his disbelieving eyes
as if the years were circling round
to desecrate the future.
He expected to die,
wanted to die,
and shut his eyes.
The icy water closed
over his head and raged
as he had once raged.
He was still now, and unafraid
even as the shock of greater
misery filled his lungs and veins
like the pills he had swallowed.
He waited in silence.

Then the rains ended.
The water began to fall.
He opened his eyes and watched it
slowly receding down his body,
exposing his skin as blank pages,
his bones as iron beams.
He picked up a bloated Bible at his feet.
Despise not the Lord, nor faint
when thou art rebuked of him:
For whom the Lord loveth he chasteneth,
and scourgeth every son whom he receiveth.
He flung the book into the night.

His reflection lay upon the water
and he saw that the rains had
dissolved the bitter factions of his former
selves, leaving him a seamless core,
a unity of truths.
He looked at the sky and saw
all his possibilities
and knew that he was free to choose.

After God

There is comfort to be had
in God's absence, just
as there is comfort in truth.

The morning sky is colder
and clearer in this light.
A bird's flight

is unencumbered by
the burden of a greater plan.
Freed from the debt

of existing we can channel
our gratitude into pride
and self-determination.

Guilt is a weed we sow
to choke the wildflowers
of freedom.

The Fire

we ignored — thought we
could ignore — was built
with supreme care.

Its flames lit
the night; its coals
warmed the years.

But when we found
ourselves unable to see
one another — only

darkness — we saw
the fire had gone, and
closed our eyes. Cold

tears hissed as they fell
into the whispering
embers. We stirred

the bed and glimpsed life;
we piled on the driest
wood

in hope. On our knees
we breathed into the ash
and smoke

and when I looked
into your eyes
I saw fire

raging
and felt the sun
burst within my heart.

The Bond

that binds the fault
is made of one part
love and the other —

faith in that love.
Morning stirs
a gentle breeze which

lifts the night and
pushes east the clouds
like so many fears and

dark thoughts.
Sunlight soothes the turgid
seam, bathes in clarity

what was once
beyond the reach of
understanding.

Flowers everywhere
spring from hope — unfolding
lush petals

fragrant as the passions
blooming deep
within the mending cracks.

Mending

for Joan; Cliff House, Bermuda

In the hospital the sun rose
pale beyond the tinted glass
and I was sealed inside,
an unhappy specimen. Here
there is nothing between
the sun and me but
a shimmering path across
the sea and a warm breeze
gentle as a lover's breath.
Ill feelings clamor out of sight,
their noise drowned out by
the more persistent surf.
The island glows in the morning
light, casting off its shadows
like my own bad dreams.
Here the light is true.

We rode our scooter to
St. George's one morning
and walked the pastel streets
in search of trinkets for our boys.
On a hill above town we visited
the century-old ruins
of an unfinished church.
Just as I had shed my faith,
so too had these crumbling walls
lost the meaning once imposed
upon them. They were free again
to be limestone, weathering the years.
I was free again to be human,
unfettered by sin.

You and I, Love, are weathering
the years. Our love is an
unfinished church. Our columns
converge under an open sky
and young trees grow at our feet.
This year has brought dark rains
upon our roofless nave
but we are strong as stone
and persistent as the sun.

Winter Study

The ornamental tree,
glazed —
the silver show —
lifts its weighted limbs to
the awakening sky.
Reflections
cascading reflections,
refractions
a regeneration of light:
this is
the sparkling
spectacle.

The Suncatcher

A simple thing:
stained glass partitioned
and arranged in an oval,
a simple shape,
lets hope stream in
in colors gay
and immutable.
A blue hummingbird,
a red flower,
green leaves;
these catch the light
and send it on
transformed into something
which stirs the mind
like music,
like life —
like love.

The Commute

The morning sun
sparkles off the trees
glazed with ice —
dazzling,
converging with
the flashy jazz
on the car radio.
Suburban streets
dressed-out, dripping
diamonds in the thaw.
I pass the glistening
headstones on the green
light and breeze
towards Watertown
Square
where
in the rear view mirror
a girl in the car behind
parts her lips
and kisses deeply
her man.
Propelled by all this
I grin and slide
as if on ice
into the office
garage.

The Music of the Spheres

In a room laced
with the warmth of a late
sun, a cello's languid strains

lift the shadows, reveal
soft connections:
gold walls patterned

by filigrees of emotion;
mahogany curved
as the measures of the minuet.

Light moves slowly
in the room, carried by phrases
which sound the spaces

between heart and mind.
Shadows deepen and stir
the objects in the room.

The cello sings in
hushed tones. The room
becomes a movement

of wood and glass,
emotion and light. The room
becomes a dance in place.

Equinox at Devereaux Beach

A man walks the shore
among the shells and glassy pools.
He absorbs the breeze,

remarks upon the gaping gulls
which hang behind like kites.
The stone in his hand is

smoother than water.
He throws it at a dissolving
wave and watches it tumble

in the weedy foam.
As he dips his hand
into the retreating surf he becomes

something of the sea and is
amazed beyond his years.
The sea swirls

around his hand as the world
swirls around its axis
which is the man.

He smiles to think the sun
and clouds are his, and what
he will tell his wife.

After the Rain

The still of a gray
dawn is broken
only by the slow
dripping of trees

lush with blossoms
and the occasional bird
tilting its head
in call to another,

and by the emergence
of slated roofs
and chimneys streaked
with the memory

of rain.
Beads of water
cling to flowers
and roll down hoods

in driveways
puddled
by glassy reflections
rippling with

the soft touch
of fallen petals.
All things
begin anew.

The Churchgoer

All I need to do is go on living.
                      —Sartre

Still wrestling with that old question,
the Churchgoer doesn't go, but stays
instead to collect his due
from the sun and choirs of trees lining
the quiet streets.

When he stops to consider the white
blossoms of the dogwood, he is mindful
of their tenuous link to the earth
from which they rose
and to which they will gently return,
one by one, at the murmured prompt
of a breeze.
He shared their fate, and the measured pace
of his progress down the walk
mirrors the progress of his years.

Distant bells recall to his mind
the dusky halls of faith, the high
colored windows staining what was clear and
true of the sun. Still, there is joy
in that wide sound, in the bright tones
of insistence, which summon the Churchgoer
to the place from which he came
and to which he may one day
return, having already divined
the answer to the question.

Three Children

at play
by the sunlit steps
of a small white
house near

a fence of red and
yellow roses —
at play
with a few small

toys, quietly
intent
squatting with bare
legs and feet,

only the girl
looking up
at the stranger
passing by

while a breeze stirs
their hair
and the curtains
in a window.

All I Need

You sit in
my lap
on the floor,
your head tucked

under my chin
in the middle
of a room filled
with music and

light — we are
father and son.
I touch
the tiny hand

in mine, the belly
round and warm,
the silken yellow
ringlets

at my cheek
and know all I
need to know,
as if

the rug beneath
us covered all
and stretched as far
as the eye can

see, leaving nothing
but you and me
in the center of this
moment.

Planing

We are
on the edge
leaning back against
the air wet
with spray, your hair
whipping and flowing
across your smile
like the water
rushing past
like the years
rushing past
since we set off,
you and I.
The masthead stirs
a vivid sky;
the sail's white wing
arcs and shivers
against the blue.
We are filled with
air and light,
feathered by the wind.
Behind us
turbulent cares
trail away,
churning off in
dark eddies
to expire in the
ever widening past.